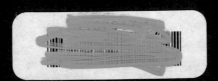

Curse
of the
Killer Hedge

David Bateman

IRON PRESS

First published 1996 by IRON Press
5 Marden Terrace, Cullercoats
North Shields, Northumberland, NE30 4PD, UK
Tel/Fax: (0191) 253 1901

Typeset by David Stephenson
in Palatino 10 point

Printed by Peterson Printers
South Shields

Cover design by Peter Mortimer and Michael Adam, including
author photos by Trisha Bell (front) and Rona Campbell (back)
The artwork for *Blake & The Tyger* is by Damian Connell

ISBN 0 906228 55 7

FIRST EDITION

IRON Press books are represented by:
Password Books Ltd.
23 New Mount Street
Manchester M4 4DE
Tel: (0161) 953 4009
Fax: (0161) 953 4001

For the Evil Dead Poets

──────ACKNOWLEDGEMENTS──────

Some of these poems have appeared in the following magazines: *Allusions,
...the buzz..., City & Guild Gazette, Flux, IRON, New Scientist, Offa's Head,
Psychopoetica, Pulpa Pulpa, Shout, Smoke, Uncompromising Positions,
Understanding, The Writer's Voice* and *Yonkly*. Also in the anthologies
*CreationEtcetera, Draft #2 Albert Poets Anthology, Evictions From The Nursery, A
Liverpool Pub* and *Verbal Abuse*; in Reprobate leaflets and in the Hybrid
booklet *From Jellybeans To Reprobation*. Some have also been broadcast on
BBC Radio Merseyside, BBC Network North West radio and Mersey
Community Radio. Thanks to all the editors concerned.

Practically all of the poems have been performed pretty widely: my
thanks to all the organizers and audiences. Especially, thanks to the long-
suffering organizers, past and present, of all the regular poetry nights in
Liverpool city centre: notably Harold Hikins, Sid Hoddes, Rona Campbell,
Mike Cunningham and Barbara Murray.

Thanks to Jean Sprackland for her help in wrangling the perverse herds
of poems; and to Peter Mortimer for his editorial taste, or lack of it.

─────David Bateman─────

was born near Sevenoaks in Kent in 1957. He received a B.Sc. in Social Studies from Teesside Polytechnic in 1979, and later received Diplomas in both Psychology and Landscape Interpretation from the University of Liverpool. He has worked as a hospital cleaner, printers' divvy, farm-worker, ecologist, coast ranger and off-licence assistant. In the 1980s he was a member of Magic Ox theatre company and also of Petra And The Probes, a rock band who were so bad that they frightened even themselves.

He appears regularly as a hardcore member of Liverpool's Evil Dead Poets; and since winning the 1990 Edinburgh Performance Poetry Competition judged by Liz Lochhead, he has also frequently been allowed out on his own, performing his poetry at pubs, clubs, schools, colleges, theatres and festivals throughout Britain. He also teaches creative writing for the University of Liverpool, and is the incompetent editor of the sporadic poetry magazine *Uncompromising Positions*.

His poems, plays, articles and stories have been broadcast on BBC and independent radio, and have appeared in numerous small magazines both too numerous and too small to mention.

His one-man shows include *From Jellybeans To Reprobation*, *The Martians Are Coming!* and *More Poems About The End Of The World (And Other Depressing Subjects)*.

Previous publications:
The Ideal God Competition (poetry) Reprobate 1989.
David Bateman's Golden Treasury Of Dinosaurs (cartoons/misinformation) Reprobate 1993.
From Jellybeans To Reprobation (poetry) Hybrid 1996.

CONTENTS

The Thrill Of The Chase

I have trained my dogs
Snoopy Timmy and
Beelzebub
to scent out the upper classes and
kill them.
Some say that this is cruel
also that the upper classes
are a good thing and
ought to be protected
being a part of our heritage and
all.
But any reasonable person I think
will admit that the upper classes
are parasites and
need to be kept down.
Snoopy Timmy and
Beelzebub
are an effective way
of doing this and
besides
I think the upper classes enjoy it.

In Your Dream...

In your dream you get mistaken
for a cargo of toxic waste
and a station official prevents
your getting off the train
at Southampton. He says that
you are not properly authorized.
You say you have a ship to meet
but he ignores all your pleas
and the train pulls out again
with you still on board. The same
happens at the next station,
then again at the next. By now
you are the only passenger
on the whole train. No station
will take you, and the train
is obliged to carry on beyond
its normal route. This is not
what the driver expected either
and he sends you messages
over the address system
to this effect. Station after
station refuses to take you,
and still the train travels on.
You half-remember a legend
of an ancient train doomed to
perpetually travel all of Britain
because of a curse on the driver.
The Flying Scotsman, that was it:
the ghost train for which all lines
become circle lines. In Cornwall
you are treated to excellent
views of St. Michael's Mount
where the Penzance line at last
reaches the coast at Marazion;
Cumbria and Wales both offer
similarly spectacular coastal views,
while the Yorkshire Dales and
Inverness-shire provide unrivalled
moorland vistas but still this

is not the holiday you had in mind.
By now most stations refuse even
to allow the train to stop,
you have become so notorious.
When snow or the wrong kind
of leaves fall on the track,
they bring in airport staff
with special hoovers and blowers
just to make sure you keep
moving. You pass public rallies
against you on station platforms.
The driver pipes radio news
reports about you through
to your carriage to the effect
that everybody would be
a lot happier if suddenly you
simply didn't exist. You wake up.
You are on a train, the same train.
You are in another version
of the same dream, the train
pulling in again at Southampton
as if for the first time.
In this version, you really
are a cargo of toxic waste
but you decide to keep quiet
about it so as not to spoil
your holiday. It won't do
any harm, you tell yourself
as you pass through the barrier.

Mixed Doubles

I dreamt that there was two of everything.
I had two places to stay
and two places to go
and two of all the usual ways of travelling between them.
It took me by surprise
and I had to think twice about it
but that was no problem.

Even couples came in couples
so when it was a toss-up between the pictures and the pub
they could do both and no trouble.
It was twelve of one and a dozen of the other.
They could even have affairs
and still be faithful at the same time.
Everything went beautifully
until I wound up in a love hexagon.
It was hard enough keeping track of my own other half
let alone my other half's own other half.
Unfortunately my other half's own other half's other half
found out what my own other half had been doing
before I did
and got together with one of my own other half's other halves'
        other half's own other half,
and came round to beat the shite out of both of me.
Fortunately I woke up at once.

Introverted

I'm sitting in this pub
with these three people
who are arguing about
how introverted they are.
They've already agreed
that introverted people
are deeper and more sensitive and stuff,
and now it only remains to be heard
who can shout loudest about
being the most introverted of all.

I tried to speak five minutes ago
but gave up.
Couldn't get a word in.

I leave them to it.
Go home and write a poem about it.
Read it out next night.
Slag them all off.
I'm really deep.
Really sensitive.

And stuff.

A Self-Made Man Of A Certain Kind

You're drinking in some local bar.
Your mate's got lost on his way to the loo,
When some fat bloke with a cheap cigar
Decides he wants to talk with you.
He talks about his business.
He talks about his wife.
He talks about his down-to-earth
Philosophy of life.

Say Hello to the self-made man.
He'll get you in a corner whenever he can.
Please say Please, and please be jealous.
He's a self-made man, and he likes to tell us:
He's a self-made man, so why aren't you, kid?
You got no plan? What are you, stupid?
He's a self-made man of a certain kind:
A self-made man with a twisted mind.

He rates his staff as pretty grim,
Cos they're not self-made men like him.
He knows what's what: he blames the unions;
Hates both Scousers and Mancunians.
He goes on package-deal safaris;
His other cars are all Ferraris;
And now he's had a few Camparis,
He can't find where his cigar is.

A cartoon sketch is all I need
To say just what you mean to me.
The crudest picture's guaranteed
To capture all your subtlety.
I could draw you with my left hand.
I could draw you in my sleep.
I could draw you underwater
Except I don't think you're that deep.

He's a self-made man with solid views
On freedom, but he won't say whose.
Thus speaks the priest of parvenues:
Some win; the rest deserve to lose.
He's a self-made man and he isn't quiet.
He's a self-made man and he needs a diet.
He's a self-made man and he won't deny it.
He's a self-made man and he likes to fly it
On a great big flag. He likes to brag.
He's a self-made man and he drives a Jag.

You Blister My Paint

I thought that love was a like a gentle rain
Like the sun up above shining down on the grain
But your kind of love must be a different strain
    I can tell you how soft & gentle you ain't
        – You blister my paint

You drive me too hard then you blame the machine
You take me apart just because you feel mean
I could do with some armoured plate in between
    I can tell you how kind & cool you ain't
        – You blister my paint

You know that I like you, you know that I care
I think you're delightful, & quite debonaire
But can you imagine the way that I feel
When my surface is cracking & starting to peel
    & I've got some bad news that I think you should know
    – You blister my paint, & it's starting to show

You got a blowtorch sun, you got an acid rain
I can feel my skin melting, away down the drain
I want to go underground & not come up again
    Let me tell you how loving & tender you ain't
        – You blister my paint
        – You blister my paint

Artistic Statement

I stand accused of preciousness
Despite my virtuosity,
By plebs who fail to realize
That the word is *preciosity*.

The herd call me a poser
But I must say I prefer
To see myself far rather
Much more as a *poseur*.

Poseurs, you'll find the crunch is,
Are far more *distingué:*
Posers move in bunches,
Poseurs in a *bouquet*.

The Day That Water Turned To Hair

One morning, from the shower spout,
Instead of water, hair came out:
Golden blonde and long and thin,
No earthly use for washing in.
And then when I went to the loo,
My pee came out more like a queue,
And though I tried till I was puffed
I could not shake that one last tuft.
There was more than enough
      to make me swear
On the day that water turned to hair.

Outside the rain was plaiting down.
We human beings crossed the town
With hairy blood inside our veins
And wondered at the hairy rains.
TV stations brought the news
From Tokyo Bay and Vera Cruz
That all the water in the world
Had gone all hairy, dry and curled.
And you couldn't get a decent cup
      of coffee anywhere
On the day that water turned to hair.

Father Thames was turning grey.
At cricket matches, hair stopped play.
Candies turned to candytufts
And Wimbledon looked more like Cruft's.
The wanton ringlets waved and spread.
All the beer had too much head.
There was nothing else to drink instead,
And no one knew why we weren't dead.
Brylcreem jumped ten points a share
On the day that water turned to hair.

The rain in Spain came down in hanks.
The Nile in Egypt flounced its banks
With floods of Andalusian swirls
While crocodiles wept their crocodile curls.
In the dark and rollered briny deep
The kraken wisely stayed asleep,
While all the oceans, lakes and brooks
Adopted stylish windblown looks.
And no one had a comb to spare
On the day that water turned to hair.

Committees met at Number Ten,
And hairdressers and weathermen
At loss to find some other way
Suggested we all start to pray.
Eternal Father, strong to save,
Protect us from this woolly grave.
For those who plough the hairy wave,
Oh won't you give the sea a shave?
Eternal Father, hear our prayer,
And please remove this excess hair.

But thunderclouds of cottonwool
Stood overhead and very full,
Prepared to loose the final storm
In hellish, hairy, hirsute form.
People swore they'd not complain
If only it would really rain,
That Nature wouldn't really send
Mankind to such a dreadful end.
But Nature must have been at lunch
        or else just didn't care
On the day that water turned to hair.

Dwarfed

Sometimes I feel
as I sit on my shelf
that my life is like
a miniature
of life itself.

I Want A Plant

What
shall I get myself
for my next birthday?
A plant.
           A houseplant.
I shall get myself a houseplant.
I want a plant to put in my flat.
I want a plant that will grow
without sunlight or heat.
I want a plant that will look after itself.
I want a plant with spikes,
                big spikes,
I want a plant with fucking great spikes,
long and sharp,
a plant that can live without leaves,
a plant that can thrive without roots,
I want a plant that can entertain my friends
when they call when I'm out.
I want a plant that can nip out to the shops
and be mistaken for me.
I want a plant that will keep me up to date.

I want a plant with spikes,
                big spikes,
I want a plant with fucking great spikes,
I want a plant that I want to look after,
I want a plant that can see to itself,
I want a plant that can live its own life,
I want a plant that will take my part
when I don't.

Reprisal Raid

We are glad to report that the raid was an unqualified success,
and that there were no civilian casualties.

*

There were a few civilian casualties which are unavoidable in
this type of operation.

*

The bombs were pin-pointed with laser accuracy onto the
military targets.

*

The children in the damaged tenements would doubtless have
grown up to become terrorists,
and you have to remember anyway that the parents do not
regard their children in the same way as we regard our own.

*

You have to remember that these people are not like us.
Their bystanders are not so innocent as our own.

*

They are a cruel people: hardly people at all.
Killing them is almost a kindness.

*

We are glad to report that the raid was an unqualified success,
hitting both its main target and a number of smaller terrorist
strongholds.

Terrorism

We must crush terrorism.
Ruthlessly.

A Damn Good Thrashing

My name is Captain Robert King,
D.S.O. (Retired),
And if a child is naughty,
then my services are hired:
For I believe in thrashing,
as my verse will plainly tell;
And if you aren't attentive,
I may demonstrate as well.

There's nothing like a damn good thrashing.
Made me what I am today.
I might look harsh with my tight moustache
But I like to look that way.

In my day all our teachers
and our parents beat us raw.
We weren't upset: I just regret
they didn't beat us more.
Folk today are going soft:
the reason they're not tough
Is that they've not had the daylights
beaten out of them enough,
But though our precious nation's
clearly going down the drain,
A judicious use of thrashing
can still make us great again
And discipline will be our salvation:
I'll raise the cane to the bums of this nation.

I've got no time for liberal fashion.
I've got the busybodies taped.
A few good stripes across those types
Will soon lick them into shape.

But first we have to catch them young,
to thrash them in their youth,
To beat their bottoms black and blue
for justice, love and truth.

For violence in the classroom
is a bane best overcome
By tough pre-emptive thrashing
with a cane across the bum;
And if at first these little thugs
persist in their disdain,
We'll tie them up with special ropes
and thrash them once again.
So up with skirts and down with trousers:
It's time to birch all the rabble-rousers.

I don't believe in false compassion.
Justice is best served rough.
As the leather cracks across their backs
They'll find they're not so tough.

For I'm a tough no-nonsense man
– I've told you that's my style –
Who believes a damn good thrashing
does us good once in a while.
Never waste the carrot:
if you're clever, use the stick.
It's half the trouble, much more fun,
and does it twice as quick.
Bring back the cat, the rod, the strap,
the sjambok and the thong,
And thrash your children daily
if you'd have them grow up strong.
It doesn't work if it doesn't hurt you:
I believe thrashing is the greatest virtue.

For there's nothing like a damn good thrashing.
Made me what I am today.
I'm the staunchest chap for the switch and strap
And I'm proud that I'm that way.

There Was A Young Pervert Called Boone...

There was a young pervert called Boone
Who exposed himself down in Rangoon.
Some men caught him flashing
And gave him a thrashing.
He's going again — very soon.

A Handsome Young Man (Bronzed Adonic)...

A handsome young man (bronzed Adonic)
Caught an illness (acute, but not chronic).
His doctor (Kildare)
Prescribed pills (and more care
In his social affairs (non-Platonic)).

Only On Fridays

There was a young fellow from Speke
Who had such a feeble physique,
On alternate Fridays
He'd manage it sideways,
Then rest for the rest of the week.

1990

That's another year gone.
Another whole year when I still didn't get a job.
I read poetry in public 59 times
& got paid for about 8 of them.
I heard from Claire at the beginning & end of the year but
    never in the middle
& wondered if, strictly speaking, my girlfriend had had to go
    to Australia.
I watched more films than I read poetry readings
& got drunk less times than that.
I narrowly avoided falling in love with the wrong person
    again
& I talked too much about the landscape of Formby.
I drank Bulgarian wine
& English beer.
I still didn't learn to dance or drive
but I did learn how to stand up & talk total nonsense to an
    audience for 27 minutes at once.
I extended my plastic dinosaur collection.
I turned one dying Busy Lizzy into two dozen thriving ones
& plotted their takeover of Liverpool 8.
I tried to read all the Famous Five books but gave up at about
    number 17.
I got worried about friends always leaving.
I worried about other things too, but that's usual.
None of the women I thought ought to have a relationship with
    me agreed.
I hitch-hiked in the sun to Edinburgh,
in the rain to London
& in the snow to Edinburgh again.
I wondered why Chief Constable James Anderton still hadn't
    been sacked.
I wrote big poems that rhymed & smaller ones about sheep
& won a prize with 3 of them.
I ate Hawaiian Crunch for breakfast
& was sad to see Thatcher fall when she did because I wanted
    to wait & see her & her party fall both at the same time.
I was famous on Hope Street
& cut my own hair by using two mirrors.

I spent most of the year at my desk & in bars.
I bought a pair of brand new jeans.
I wasn't very good at recognizing plants when I should have
      been
but I finished my dissertation with blistered fingers & 3 hours
      to spare.
I tried to harden myself against the insincerity of friends
& my boots kept on getting full of sand from Formby dunes.
I earnt £225 in one week
& nothing in most of the others.
I gashed my leg on the microphone stand at the Playhouse
      while pretending to be a bouncing bomb
but otherwise enjoyed good health.
Neither the museum nor the library required my services.
I ate more curries than I read poetry readings
but not quite as many as I watched films.
I thought of Claire every time I ate olives.
I took no photographs,
but my head is full of pictures.
I don't suppose it was a bad year.
I can see it had its moments.
But some years you want to forget singing Auld Lang Syne &
      just pat each other on the back on making it through to the next one,
& 1990 was one of those.

Four Detrital Haiku

Slugs are communing
on the bin-bag in the rain:
they think they've found God.

Her grin's ironic:
she's been dead two thousand years
and has perfect teeth.

Sad years of chances
wasted: a pack of condoms
past their use-by date.

The guest who won't leave:
smoking your cigarettes, and
missing the ashtray.

This Poem

Consider this poem as your undiscovered adultery,
your fingers in the cash-box.
Better keep quiet about this dangerous little poem.

Underwater

It only happened once,
the dream that everything was underwater.
It must have been when he was thirteen,
twelve even; but the idea stayed,
grew throughout the next year or so
of pointless school, of buses, parks
and X-certificate Sunday dinners.
It was hard to forget that for maybe five minutes
his homeland had become the bed
of a dreamt ocean,
hard to forget the slow viscous fluttering of oak leaves,
branches swaying in the new currents
of a silent green world.

Revisions and Third Year exams came and went.
Friends remained ready to turn into enemies
at half a moment's notice.

Sitting amongst strangers
on the darkened pews
of his compulsory Confirmation class,
and while the vicar talked of John the Baptist,
he would secretly turn the pages instead
to the other John's visions of earthquake,
fire, brimstone and blood;
but still, overall, he preferred his own version.
Swimming above the tree-tops, he'd seen the buildings
of submerged suburbia and the city beyond,
swum through its silent streets like submarine canyons,
swum up over the roofs,
swum high over the winding bed
of the drowned river,
and never once wondering where all the people had gone.

Cornered again against the playground prison fence
by his Fourth Year so-called friends,
he managed, as they grabbed his arms and legs,
to get one hopeful look at his watch,
but this time he wasn't saved by the bell.

Later, giving up on homework
in a home full of arguments,
brothers, sisters, parents,
he instead traced the coastline of his island nation
from his school atlas,
but drawing the line at one hundred metres above sea level.
That done, he took a fresh piece of paper
and drew a fresh coastline
at two hundred metres.
On later days he raised the sea level yet higher,
watching the coast move ever further inland,
seeing how the shape of the country
changed slowly at first,
a chunk lost here, a chunk there,
but then quickly lost its identity
to a scattered archipelago.
– What are you doing?
– It's an exercise for school.
These islands in turn became smaller,
shrinking with each hundred metre step
till the waters closed satisfyingly over their heads
leaving a blank page.
While brothers and sisters fought over TV channels,
he turned his attention to maps of the world.

Each morning, he cycled his newspaper-round,
and his schoolwork, as ever, was unworthy of remark:
you try to keep your head down;
act as if everything's alright.

In classrooms of varnished wood and dull blackboard,
he would let the voice at the front drift away,
see the splashing of the first small wavelets
licking and pawing at the building's foot
almost as if they were tame,
then watch the tide slowly climb each outside wall
turning all the school's colours to muted shades of green.
Ground-floor doorways would flop open like sluices
to welcome the flow:
the school beneath him became a giant swimming pool
now mysteriously empty of people,
a swimming pool of dining hall, office and drowned furniture.

And still the waters would rise,
slowly filling the stairwells,
spilling up onto landings,
creeping along corridors,
filling the corridors and then moving on,
rising through the school's interior
with a smooth precision
towards the classroom where he sat.
At first, no one would notice
the slowly spreading puddle by the door,
and when they did, they'd stifle their snickers,
secretly prodding each other and pointing,
thinking it all a practical joke
until the teacher, at last noticing the growing pool,
happened to glance out of the window;
and by then it would be too late for all of them.

One lunchtime,
trapped yet again against the corner of the high wire fence
by his so-called friends,
he silently wished for the oceans
to rise up and cover everything.

Shadow

And still the shadow uncast
in the corner of my room
grows larger.

To ask why seems pointless:
in some corner of my mind,
I already know.

Haiku

for Gregory Corso

Birds are friendly spies
singing their reports to trees
who ponder gravely.

A Guide To Flying

Flying is simple and fun.
If you can't fly, this poem tells you how to.
If you have already flown, I hope that this poem will encourage
you to fly more often.

You want to fly.
All you need to know about flying can be covered under the
headings of running, jumping and swimming.
Most important is swimming, and we will deal with this first.
If you are not already a swimmer, then it is probably best to
begin by learning to swim.
A number of popular guides are widely available which can help
you with this part.
Having learnt to swim in the water, simply do the same in the
air.
You are now flying.

If however you experience any initial problems in swimming
through the air, it is worth knowing that you can achieve a
similar effect when everywhere you know is flooded.
It is probably best not to deliberately flood the whole world
merely for this purpose, but it can sometimes happen that
everywhere you know is now underwater anyway, and it is
worth making the most of these opportunities.
You should not encounter any problems in breathing underwater, but this is largely a matter of confidence, and some
people may find they experience a little difficulty at first.
A bigger problem, though, is visibility: water during global
flooding is seldom as clear as ordinary air; and there is also a
tendency for everyone else in the world to mysteriously disappear.

Much better, then, to avoid wholesale flooding altogether, and
simply to swim in the air in more normal conditions.
Even non-swimmers can learn to fly by learning to swim in the
air in the first place instead of in water.
There are those people who never learnt to swim because they
were afraid of getting water up their nose or in their eyes.
When you are learning to swim in the air, these problems
simply never occur. You can learn to fly with a confidence

you never had in the water.
It can, however, be difficult for a beginner simply to fly from
a standing position, and this is where running and jumping
come in.
Jumping is undoubtedly the simplest and easiest way of taking
off, so this is an important element in learning to fly.
Begin by making quite small jumps, then practise by jumping
and staying up for longer and longer periods.
Use your arms to help keep you up.
Eventually you will find that you don't come down at all: you
are now treading air, and you are free to fly in any direction
you choose.
You can fly higher and look down over the rooftops or the
trees.

You can go in a bee-line to your friend's house.
You can have telepathy as you fly towards someone you love
(but this is a large area, and is covered fully in a separate
poem).

If you have any problems in jumping higher and higher, you
may find it useful to pick out nearby objects or people that
you would like to jump over.
Try jumping as high as someone's head, then maybe a playground fence or a castle wall, or perhaps a nearby tree.

Running is another useful way of getting started in flying.
As you run, gradually take longer and longer strides till finally
your feet never touch the ground at all, and you are flying.
Remember to use your arms.
One of my own ways of taking off by running is to run faster
and faster, leaning further and further forward all the while
till my hands can easily touch the ground if I want and I am
almost horizontal, and I begin swimming almost at ground
level, gradually gaining height from there.

As you practise, you will soon find your own preferred ways
of taking off, as well as developing your own favourite strokes
for actually flying.

When you are learning to fly, do not be surprised if sometimes
you find that your home city has changed around you, or

that the landscape you were born in has become barely
recognizable.

These changes only mean that there is so much more to
explore.

If, for example, the walls have lost their windows and rear up
like blind sandstone around you, so much the more reason
to step up from the ground and tread the rooftop air: up here
there is more land and more sky; here there is blue and brown
to move around between as you please.

Fly to that friend's house.

Fly to that someone you love.

Look around at all that land below you.

Look around at all that sky.

An A-Z Of Why I Hate Mornings

(A tirade)

I hate my mornings.
I hate my mornings
with an A because they're awful
with a B because they're buggerawful
with a C because they're callous
with a D because they're depressing
with an E because they're early (*too* early)
with an F because they're fuckawful
with a G because they're godawful
with an H because they're hellish
with an I because they're idiotic
with a J because they're jaded, & a joke (a bad one),
      & jealous of oblivion
with a K because they're Kafkaesque
with an L because they're lonely
with an M because they're miserable
with an N because they're nauseous
with an O because they're *obligatory*
with a P because they're pissawful
with a Q because they're *quintessentially* awful
with an R because they're rough (just when I need
      treating gently)
with an S because they're *smelly*
with a T because they're tiresome
with a U because they're unbearable
with a V because they're vile
with a W because they're wearisome
with an X because they're Xanthippic (that means bitchy,
      & you can look it up if you want to)
with a Y because they're yucky
& with a Z because they're zombie-like.
Afternoons are a fuck of a sight better.
I don't mind those at all.

One Of The Problems That I Always Find With English Absurdist Poetry

One of the problems that I always find with English absurdist
poetry is the proliferation of queens.
100 queens.
There: look at that. A hundred queens in this poem already.
That's even worse than usual. I wouldn't mind if it weren't
for the fact that they're so expensive to keep. I mean, who
can afford to look after a hundred queens these days?
200 queens.
Two hundred queens?
Yes, 200 queens.
Is that inclusive of the previous hundred queens?
Yes.
Oh. Right. That's not quite so bad as it might have been,
then... As I was saying: who can afford to look after a
hundred queens these days, let alone two hundred queens?
The Société Anglaise de la Poésie Absurde isn't taking any
more, and the R.S.P.C.A. won't touch them either. Is it
any wonder that absurdist poetry is going through a low
period?
800 queens.
Eight hundred queens?! What happened to *four* hundred?
Your last line was overly long.
Oh. I see... Anyway, to continue: is it any wonder that most
absurdist poems are so bloody short these days? I mean,
who can afford to write long absurdist poems?
1,600 queens.
Oh, I've had enough of this. I shall take them down to London
and sell them to American tourists before the market gets
swamped completely. And even then, I'll be surprised if I
even manage to cover the transport costs. I mean, queens
are ten a penny these days.
6,400 queens.
Oh, blast.

The Bodyguard's Tale

Venerable Chögyam Trungpa, eleventh Trungpa Tulku,
chosen reincarnation of ten previous Trungpa Tulku,
supreme abbot of the Surmang monasteries of Jye Kundo,
teacher of the Kagyü sect and the ancient N'yingma,
one day to test the alertness of his bodyguards,
attempted to throw himself down the staircase
as we walked beside him at the Naropa Institute.
Taken by surprise, we failed to catch him,
watching helplessly as he fell and landed on his head.
Afterwards, we picked him up, reassured him
and drove him to the hospital for checks,
which showed him not much the worse for his fall.

Religion may give meaning to an empty man's life,
and tradition may give him authority.
Teaching can get you a job if you're lucky,
and if you have money, it may buy respect,
but even a team of specially-appointed bodyguards
can't save you from being a complete asshole.

Chernobyl: The Musical
(Excerpts)

Our Nuclear Reactor's Ignition...

Our nuclear reactor's ignition
Led us into a crisis condition.
   Did the management stand?
   No, they ran like hell, and
Left a note on the door: GONE FISSION.

Singeing In The Rain

Don't eat your sandwiches out in the rain.
You'll only get radiation sickness again.
It's a risk you can't afford to take,
So stay indoors in your lunch-break.

There Was A Young Man From Llanfairpwllgwyngyllgogerychwyrndrobwll-llantysiliogogogoch...

There was a young man from Llanfairpwllgwyngyllgogerych-
    wyrndrobwllllantysiliogogogoch
With a trans-Menai-Strait-travelling cock.
    From his home he could screw with
    His girl in Bontnewydd;
That happy young man from Llanfairpwllgwyngyllgogerych-
    wyrndrobwllllantysiliogogogoch.

Look Back In Bangor

Where rich folk make their second home
In Cymru's hills I like to roam
And watch the work of arsonists
Glow gently through the evening mists.

A Concrete Parthenon In Nashville, Tennessee

The Parthenon – a temple dedicated to the goddess Athena Parthenos – was built on the Akropolis at Athens around 440 B.C., under the rule of General Perikles. A long time later, in 1896, on the other side of the Atlantic Ocean, the state of Tennessee was celebrating its centennial anniversary. In the state capital, Nashville, they knew just what to do...

O citizens of Nashville
come and listen to my plea
to put the gem upon the crown
of Nashville's jubilee.
Down here between the abattoirs
and boatyards we all know,
we need something extra special
we can always have on show.
What we need is an old Greek temple here
that the folks can come and see.
We're gonna build a concrete Parthenon
in Nashville, Tennessee.

I saw it once in Athens
and it sure looked mighty fine.
I drew up a purchase contract
but the natives wouldn't sign.
But that's their own misfortune
and damn them all to hell,
cos they can keep theirs where it is
and we'll have one as well.
Yes, if Perikles can do it
then I don't see why can't we.
We're gonna build a concrete Parthenon
in Nashville, Tennessee.

Now, London has its Tower,
and China has its Wall,
and Egypt has its famous crypts
but Nashville's got fuck-all.
And all across the U.S.A.
the story's all the same:
a puny pueblo here and there
and we know who's to blame.
We've been let down very badly
by the Sioux and Cherokee,
so we're gonna build a concrete Parthenon
in Nashville, Tennessee.

They built so many palaces
and temples in Peru,
you'd think the Incas can't have had
all that much else to do.
And don't you know in Mexico
there's pyramids to spare
and all those greedy greasers
just sit back and gloat and stare.
All the spiks have ancient monuments
so why can't you and me?
We deserve that concrete Parthenon
in Nashville, Tennessee.

There's a Muse amongst the cotton-mills
and even Zeus is thrilled
at all the fluted columns
and the statues that we'll build.
We'll make our own Akropolis
down in Centennial Park,
and with floodlights all around
it'll sure look pretty after dark.
And how vast our plaster-cast
Athena Parthenos will be,
when we build our concrete Parthenon
in Nashville, Tennessee.

They say that we're uncultured.
Well, this should shut their mouth,
and someday soon they'll call this town
the Athens of the South.
So mix that sand and that cement,
and mix it up real good,
and we'll have a hunk of history here
in our own neighborhood.
Here's a problem for the Joneses
that they didn't quite foresee.
We're gonna build a concrete Parthenon
in Nashville, Tennessee.

A New Guide To Stonehenge

Accidentally deep-frozen for over three thousand years, a neolithic man recently disc-
overed in an ice-floe at Rhyl proved, upon being thawed, to be alive and well. Following a
crash course in modern English, he explained that he had been paddling on the beach when
overtaken by a cold snap.

Surprised by some of the changes that had occurred to Britain in the intervening period,
but nevertheless quick to adapt, he soon found gainful employment in Wiltshire...

Of course, all this used to be shops.
Oh yes: biggest indoor market for miles around.
Quite modern in its time, too:
all those neat, clean lines;
the great stones standing there
in their bold primary colours.
Yeah: pity about the paintwork.
Could do with a bit of brightening up again, really.
Still, one thing about grey:
it goes with anything.
Must say, I preferred it the old way, though.
Some people complained, of course:
said it was a monstrosity;
said it messed up the skyline,
sitting in the middle of the plain like that.
But if you wanted to swop a few antler picks
for some decent stone tools,
this was the place to come.
Thinking about it it,
I'm surprised they don't do it up
and re-open it.
Plenty of customers about,
especially with that new road nice and handy now.
Shame about the roof, though.
I always said that roof would go for a burton one day.
It always did leak something rotten.
What? Sunrise and moonrise?
Oh yes: quite correct.
Never went in for all that astronomical stuff myself, though:
used to leave that to the experts.
Never came here at night except for a couple of circuses.
If you ask me, it was probably the tight-rope walking that did
for a couple of those uprights.

Not guyed properly, I'd say.
Still, at least none of them ever actually fell on the audience as
        far as I know,
and it was always a good gig:
nice performance space and lots of room for the juggling and
        fire-breathing.
Yes, of course we had fucking fire by then, you wally.
Big audiences, too.
The Maiden Castle mob would be up from Dorset
and my lot would be down from Windmill Hill.
After the circus we'd have a right knees-up.
What? Mystic trances?
I'll say. We got tranced out of our heads every chance we got.
That's where the precise alignment of the stones comes in,
        because otherwise most of us would probably never have
        got home afterwards.
I still don't remember how I ended up in Rhyl.

Curse Of The Killer Hedge

*(The tragic tale of a young woman who goes out across the countryside
at night to meet her lover and is killed by a hedge.)*

I am going out.
I am going out across the countryside at night
tonight to meet my lover.

I am wearing my special shoes.
My bum is as beautiful as jewels,
my belly is like a wheatsheaf wrapped in flowers
and my breasts are bouncing like bouncy deer.

I am going out.
I am hurrying along dark country roads.
My lover has not called
and I'm feeling really rash.

Like a bundle of myrrh is my lover to me:
he shall lie all night between my breasts.
He is majestic as the mighty Pennines
with their towering Ash trees.
His name is David Bateman
and he is altogether the sexiest bastard between Land's End
        and John O'Groats.
His thighs are columns of alabaster
set in sockets of gold.
His belly is bright as marble
overlaid with sapphires.
His nose is shaped most wonderfully like Formby Point
and his hairline is dignified and mature.

I am hurrying.
I am hurrying to see my lover.
I am hurrying between dark hedges that almost seem to close
        in on me
as I hurry past.

I especially don't like the look of that particular bit of hedge
        just coming up,
but that's silly, isn't it?

Oh! Oh! The hedge has attacked me,
clutching me in its horrible thorny grasp.
Oh! Oh!
Hedge, let me go
at once!
But though I struggle
and though I kick against the hedge with my special shoes,
my arms become thornily thorn-entangled
and my shoes take root in the hedgebank soil.
My bouncy deer are trapped by thorns,
my jewels are turned thorn berries,
my wheatsheaf becomes a stem of thorns
wrapped in thorn flowers.
I am hedge-ate,
trunk and limb.
I am hedge-ate
and turned to hedge.
This is all that stupid bastard Bateman's fault
for not being on the phone.

I am waiting.
I stand here softly rustling in the dark and quiet countryside.
I am waiting for my lover,
and I'm going to turn that bastard into a hedge too next time
  he comes this way.

The Comet

Sparkle, sparkle, little comet!
How you make me want to vomit!
There must be, in your metallurgy,
Stuff to which I have an allergy.

Celestial Music, Large Astral Bodies,
And Words For Other Worlds

I like to watch The Sky At Night,
To gaze upon the astral zone,
And hear the music of the spheres
With Patrick Moore on xylophone.

Tinkle, tinkle! Patrick Moore
Hits the blocks and grits his jaw.
"Help me, O thou Sun and Moon,
And get me safely through this tune."

*

Now Patrick Moore's a star of stars,
But though he's big, I can't conclude
If he or maybe Russell Grant
Has quite the biggest magnitude.

If Russell Grant and Patrick Moore
– Assuming both to be compliant –
Were placed adjacent on one floor,
'Twould form a double supergiant.

*

From stars beneath Orion's belt
To Saturn's moons, like Rhea and Janus,
Patrick Moore knows how it's spelt
But still he can't pronounce Uranus.

To say "Your Anus" isn't done:
It tickles thoughts impure in us;
So Patrick Moore avoids this pun
And calls the planet "Urinous."

Blake & The Tyger

William Blake
Rarely makes a mistake,
But I do wish he'd try
Spelling 'tiger' without a 'y'.

'Tyger'? 'Tyger' with a 'y'
Is not found in my diction'ry.
Other mortals get it right.
You'd think that Blake the poet might.

Genesis: A Summary

At the start, God created the lot,
Then told Adam and Eve what was what.
    There was strife between brothers;
    Some folk begat others;
And there I lost track of the plot.

Bond. Basildon Bond

The pen is mightier than the sword:
A point most aptly underscored
By James Bond's special cannon-pen
As used in Never Say Never Again.

Clerihew Clerihew

Edmund Clerihew Bentley
Worked most intently
Writing whimsical biographical quatrains at home in his
    mansion
With snappy rhymes but crappy scansion.

T. S. Eliot

T. S. Eliot
Sailed upon a very smelly yacht
From America all of the way to Great Britain
And then proceeded to concoct some of the most incomprehen-
    sible poetry ever written.

"MACULATE" Scores Eighty-Nine

1
Even as a poet
T. S. Eliot still maintained
the consistently high word scores
made possible by a lifetime of international Scrabble
using only long words wherever at all possible
and making sure that any smaller words
had plenty of Zs, Qs, Js
Xs and Ks.

2
He would
have scored even higher
if he hadn't lost so many turns
for improper use of proper nouns and were it not
for his odd and regrettably incomprehensible habit
of trying to write his poems
in several languages
at once.

3
This is the
way the world ends.
This is the way the world ends.
This is the way the world ends. Not with a bang
but a whimper

with the M
on a double letter score
and the W on a triple word score
makes sixty and then adding on the fifty point bonus
for using up all of his last seven letters in one go
gives a massive one hundred and ten.
Εατ σζιτ, μοτθερφυχκερ,
he remarks.

The Cautionary Tale Of
Patience Frail

*WHO WAS CURSED WITH THE SIN OF ANGER,
AND SO DIED BY EATING A TELEVISION*

Patience Frail, of Frailty Hall,
Had several faults when she was small,
The chiefest of these being that
She was a spoilt and loathsome brat,
A selfish, mean, conceited, smug,
Ill-tempered, vicious little thug.

Her father, Sir Jerome (yes, *him*)
Would pander to her every whim,
And meanwhile Lady Henrietta,
If anything, was worse, not better,
Preferring to ignore her child,
Who subsequently ran quite wild,

And did those things she should not do:
Like kicking cats, and hamsters too;
Like stealing sweets and treats and toys
From all the local girls and boys;
Like stamping on her granny's glasses
And sneering at the Lower Classes.

Now these are most unpleasant tricks,
Quite shocking in a child of six,
And Patience's precocious pranks
Like robbing local shops and banks
Caused top police to gently chasten
Sir Jerome (another Mason),

Who promised he would slap her wrist.
(He did so the next day, but missed.)
But, for all her many faults,
Like battery and armed assaults
The one which sealed her sorry fate
Was anger, as I'll now relate.

One evening, in her seventh year,
As Patience sat with parents near,
And watched the football on the box
And irritably chewed her socks,
She threw them down and cried, "I'm bored!
It's minutes now since someone scored."

She changed the channels, tried a few,
And finding nothing that would do,
She cursed and spat and stamped and swore
And then tried changing sides some more.
She butted buttons, kicked the cat.
(Her father said, "Please don't do that.")

In grimly growing fury, Patience
Wildly switched between the stations
Till in a rage quite unconfined
A need for vengeance seized her mind:
She shouted out her rash decision:
"I'm going to eat that television!"

Her father, with his gentle tact,
Now cautioned her against this act.
"It's bad for you, my dear," he said,
"To eat things bigger than your head."[1]

The wisdom of her father's plea
Had no effect on Patience. She
began with the remote control
And this she quickly swallowed whole,
Then did her very best to get
Her teeth around the T.V. set.

The T.V. was by no means small,
But step by step she forced it all
Inside her mouth, then in her spite
Bit down on it with all her might.

Alas, as she bit down, a boom
And fearful flash filled all the room,
And when at last the smoke had cleared
Both child and set had disappeared
(Except for bits of both now peeling
Gently from the bloodied ceiling).

The undertakers, Digg & Pitts,
When called to gather up the bits,
Could not tell with great precision
Patience from the television,
And not to be accused of sloth,
They gathered up and buried both.

Henrietta and Jerome
Both shed a tear, then went back home
And, facing up with brave endurance,
Made a claim on the insurance,
Consoled themselves with cups of tea,
And ordered their brand new T.V.

MORAL:
Reader, let us now dispense
With niceties. For sheer good sense,
One simple rule cannot be beaten:
T.V. should be seen, not eaten.

[1] *A quip I stole without a care*
   From I-can't-quite-remember-where.

ANIMAL LOVE

High Wire Act

A corgi of wondrous agility
Possessed a most useful facility.
From the flying trapeze
He'd mount Great Danes with ease:
A trick he'd picked up from nobility.

Mingus (being *Probably The Western World's First Ever Rude Poem About Aardvarks*)

A sensitive aardvark called Mingus
Found foreplay hard work with no fingers.
But his praises are sung,
For his fourteen-inch tongue
Gives his ladies a pleasure that lingers.

Flexibility

The worms, being hermaphroditic,
Find each other's sex catalytic,
And can swing either way
Without once being gay,
Which baffles the prude and the critic.

The Fine Art Of Humping

Learner drivers should study the case
Of the camel's manoeuvering grace.
  As they screw back-to-back
  They soon master the knack
Of reversing into a tight place.

Prawn King Abdicates

At a krill-breeding farm I won't name,
A king-stud who tired of his fame
  Said "The sex is okay,
  But I don't like the way
That I'm only a prawn in their game."

Extremely Deep Throat*

While fellating her lover one day,
Madame Spoonworm got carried away,
  And she swallowed him whole
  Just as he reached his goal:
You might say he was coming to stay.

* The female of Bonellia, a species of spoonworm, is up to 20,000 times the size of the male; and the males do indeed often live *inside* the female. So the ending is a happy one. Isn't nature wonderful.

Snail Tale

Two snails, in their keen copulation,
Went a week with no sign of cessation.
    On the eighth day he came
    And was heard to exclaim
"Drat! A premature eejaculation!"

Angle Poise

Two angler-fish, while they were screwing
In the aquarium, saw people viewing.
    With a kiss to each snout
    They turned both their lights out;
Then they got on with what they'd been doing.

At The Zoo

Camel looks smugly,
smugly at we,
as we stand watching Camel:
Janet and me.

Tell me, O Camel,
as you stand in this zoo:
Why the smugness? You've got
some explaining to do.

Sex is the answer,
I see in your eye:
you think you've got one over
on Janet and I.

I see in your sneering
your smug claim that you
and your mate can do it backwards
and often do.

Well, that may be so
if the rumours are true,
but we'll find out who's got
one over on who.

So if you fetch your mate
and begin to caress,
meanwhile Janet and I will
each other undress.

Bonus points will be scored
for all variation,
satisfaction derived, and for
prolongation.

Just ignore passers-by
and I'll now start the count:
Six. Five. Four. Three.
Onyourmarks! Getset! Mount!

So we made love on the pathway
  and we made love on the bench.
We made love in the meadow
  and made love against the fence.
We made love at every angle,
  every push and squirm and kiss
and as we made love up a tree
  I called, "I bet you can't do this!"

As we made love more and more
  we left the camels far behind.
We left them standing from the start
  and now we'd beat them blind.
But it was still too early
  for our love-making to stop,
so we made love at the aviary,
  aquarium, and shop.

We made love by the bear-pit
  and the tigers and the quails,
and climaxed at the ape-house
  amidst anthropoidal wails.
But as we two, in afterplay,
  swang on the ape-trapeze,
a voice called up to call us down,
  and said, "It's the police."

Policeman looks oddly,
oddly at we.
"You'd best put on your clothes
and then come along with me."

Camel looks smugly,
knows that we've been bested:
camels do it in public, and
don't get arrested.

When The Holy Ghost Came, Say Traditions...

When the Holy Ghost came, say traditions,
Mary acted without inhibitions.
    She had God on her side,
    And then had him astride,
And in several other positions.

Spiritual Love

In the case of the mad mystic, Ilya,
The shrink diagnosed spectrophilia:
    He summoned phantasms
    And reached his orgasms
By – well, being over-familiar.

A Student Psychiatrist Named Ray...

A student psychiatrist named Ray
Found he'd passed his exams with an A.
    He was so pleased and glad,
    He went totally mad,
And he had to be taken away.

A Pathetic Young Fool Used To Hector Me...

A pathetic young fool used to hector me
With his schemes which seemed quite incorrect to me.
    He planned, in his gloom,
    To return to the womb,
But was foiled by his mum's hysterectomy.

The Food Of Love

"Jim, you're drunk!" she said: "That's the last straw!"
And stormed out through the takeaway door.
    With tears in his eyes,
    He ate both of their pies,
And was lovesick all over the floor

There Was A Young Purist Called Pughsley...

There was a young purist called Pughsley
Who dined upon wholefoods and mughsley.
    At times he took breaks
    And ate massive great steaks,
But that wasn't what he did ughsley.

L'Exhibitionism

There was a young lady from Leicester
And a curious longing obseicester,
To show all of Towcester
Her parts nethermowcester;
It's a shame that they came to arreicester.

Algolagnia (or I thought that algolagnia was an Italian meal until I discovered bondage and discipline)

You may find, if you try algolagnia,
That your husband just don't understagnia
And he curls up his lips
At your leather and whips.
Still, you can't expect everything, cagnia?

My Diction Goes Wrongly Syntaxative...

My diction goes wrongly syntaxative
And my wordage is holy intraxative.
I think that I fear
I have verbal dire-rear
But it may be I'm merely dyslaxative.

Stardom

1: A Medical Opinion

Doctor Hartwig has a sign in his office
that says
JUST BECAUSE YOU'RE PARANOID
IT DOESN'T MEAN
THEY'RE NOT TRYING TO GET YOU.
His sincerity however
is open to doubt
since he claims not to believe
in my voices,
dismissing them as symptoms
rather than causes.
Look,
I say to him,
people really are saying terrible things about me
behind my back,
I can prove it to you.
And so saying
I empty my carrier-bagful
of Sunday newspapers
onto his desk.
Pictures of me look up accusedly at him
from their headline cages,
meshes of words describing
everything from drunkenness and tax fraud
to bad acting and kinky sex with aliens,
usually from Venus.
It's all lies,
I tell him,
especially about the Venusians,
I never had sex with a Venusian in my life,
I hate Venusians,
it's the Venusians that started all this
and now they've turned even the
press and television against me,
the papers used to love me,
and now they're doing this.

Yes,
says Doctor Hartwig
understandingly,
but just because they really are
trying to get you
it doesn't mean you're not paranoid.

2: Making The Cowboy Movie

Voices, voices,
always voices in my head
like waves of arrows
fired from all directions,
deadly red Indians
behind each cactus.

How can a man do
whatever a man's got to do
with all these voices
always talking,
slipping poison
in the beans and coffee?

Voices circle round my head
like vulture cries above the pass
till all at once
the echoes vanish:
silence settles
like an ambush.

I don't like it.
It's too quiet.

3: On "Vacation"

Come on out. We know you're in there.

Of course I am in here.
Seeing as I am not in the day room;
seeing as I am not in my own room;
seeing as the little revolving sign
says (presumably)
NGAGED V rather than D VACANT;
and seeing as the staff in any case
can see (beneath the lower edge of the door)
my shoes and crumpled trousers
as I sit on the toilet bowl,
I would have thought it fairly obvious
that I am in here.

You can't stay in there forever, you know.

On the inside of the cubicle door,
facing me squarely as I sit on the bowl,
someone has inscribed this graffito:
    Hilary, Hilary, nursing auxiliary,
    How does your mental ward do?
    With manic yells from padded cells,
    And paranoids all in a queue.

I see this as being in very poor taste,
especially as the last line
is very obviously referring to me.

4: Out Patient

Three tablets a day
keep the voices away.
Jolly good,
you're definitely progressing now,
says Doctor Hartwig one morning.

At the time I hide my doubts, but
afterwards I'm still unconvinced.
Now I don't hear the voices
how will I know what
they're plotting against me?

5: Postscript

Since my retirement from the movies
Doctor Hartwig says that my paranoia
is in spontaneous remission
and laments the equally spontaneous
appearance of my freshly acquired
anxiety neurosis.

And though these days life is quiet,
one new worry has come to call:
that perhaps no one
is talking about me
behind my back
at all.

How Do They Do It?

I'd like to know the how and why,
In slushy romance picture shows,
They cry and cry and cry and cry,
Yet never have to blow their nose.

Let's Go Back To Your Childhood

Your life is full of problems:
Well, that's no cause for shame.
And things have got too much for you:
Well, everyone's the same.

So now let's find what's left your mind
So twisted, bent and lame.
Let's go back to your childhood
And find out what's to blame.

You're feeling frustrated yet strangely elated:
You're manic-depressive for sure.
That you have a latent psychosis is patent
And could be quite tricky to cure.

Your symptoms are riches of tics and of twitches,
Of worries and fears, big and small.
You just can't relax for your panic attacks.
It's a wonder you function at all.

Your sense of defeatment just cries out for treatment.
Your spirit's too faint to locate.
Can psychoanalysis cure this paralysis?
Is it already too late?

Is there one simple cause for your psychotic flaws?
Or are you as mad as a hatter?
Well, first you should know that these symptoms you show
Are only the tip of the matter.

Your id has twisted inwards
And your ego's quite inert.
You'd make the shyest wallflower
Look like an extrovert.

We need to find the causes,
So though the cure might hurt,
Let's go back to your childhood
And dig up all the dirt.

A neurotic defence against childhood events
Often leaves an emotional scar,
And it's these that traumatically, psychosomatically,
Made you the wreck that you are.

As you sat on your potty, a poodle called Spotty
Once barked very slightly, or less,
And now you're psychotically anal-erotic
Which tends to account for the mess.

But the anal fixation's reaction formation
Has made you exceedingly mean;
And the potty, it's clear, now accounts for the fear
That you have for all things coloured green.

When your phobia spread to all things coloured red,
It turned you right in on yourself.
You became narcissistic and most masochistic,
And hence the decline in your health.

You had some gross encounters
Of the id-cathexis kind.
You thought that you'd suppressed them all
And left your past behind.

But now things don't look quite so good
Within your twisted mind,
So let's go back to your childhood
And see what we can find.

Your problems all come from your love for your mum
And your father you wanted to kill.
It's perfectly plain that you've never been sane
And there's hardly a hope that you will.

Your dreams about fish show an unconscious wish,
A desire to return to the womb,
Which you might as well stop since your mum's had an op,
And there certainly isn't the room.

Your obsessive belief that you're losing your teeth
Of course relates straight to your dad,
For you hold him to blame when the tooth-fairy came
And he smashed the illusions you'd had.

You hated your brother you once tried to smother:
A fact you refuse to admit,
So your hate is displaced to the whole human race,
And this doesn't help one little bit.

   Your thoughts are all so negative
   You can't see through the murk.
   You've an id of which you should get rid
   And a psyche that doesn't work.

   You're a problem personality:
   What some folks call a jerk.
   So let's go back to your childhood
   And see what horrors lurk.

You've an ego-ideal that's completely unreal
And you've no super-ego at all.
It's vividly graphic you're quite psychopathic
And have been since you were quite small.

Your unconscious thoughts are the most sordid sorts
That most adults left with their teddy.
It's a wonder, in fact, you're so totally cracked,
That you've not been committed already.

When you were teeny yer got schizophrenia;
Split personality, too;
Suppressed satyriasis; hypochondriasis;
Paranoias all in a queue.

You've got all the complexes of both of the sexes
Mixed up in a Freudian knot,
And while your libido's mixed up with your ego,
Your id is mixed up with the lot.

Your mind is full of weirdness
And your brain's begun to rot.
It's obvious there's more to this,
But heaven knows just what.

But time's up now; come back next week,
Lay your money on the spot,
And we'll go back to your childhood
And see what else you've got.

A Singer Who Came From Milano...

A singer who came from Milano
Had privates made out of Meccano.
   He sang bass-tenor, but
   By unscrewing one nut
He could also reach mezzo-soprano.

'Twas A Chemist Who Let Young Melissa In...

'Twas a chemist who let young Melissa in
On the trick of home-made nitroglycerine.
   They found bits of Milly
   From Cyprus to Scilly;
Larissa's the city they'll miss 'er in.

The Dashing Adonis Of Killin... *

The dashing Adonis of Killin
Said, "Find me a bowl to be ill in,"
For his trusted Venus
Of virtuous cleanness
Now told him he'd need penicillin.

* Others may prefer:

The Vibrant Young Venus Of Killin...

The vibrant young Venus of Killin
Said, "Find me a bowl to be ill in,"
For she'd not seen the lowness
Of her brave Adonis
Till finding she'd need penicillin.

Dear Editor

If you want to stay healthy, take this tip
And put down that rejection slip.
We know you've always had good taste,
And hurting people is such a waste:
So send us an acceptance.
Just send us an acceptance.
That's all you have to do.
We don't like breaking editors' legs,
But sometimes we have to,
You see,
Sometimes we just have to.

We like to see our work in print.
We know that you can take a hint,
So editor, consider sweetly
On these verses typed so neatly:
You're bound to like some of it.
You're bound to like some of it,
Just like we like you.
We don't like breaking editors' legs,
But sometimes we have to,
Sadly,
Sometimes we just have to.

Take care

David Bateman (and his mates)

If Poetry Was Water...

If poetry was water
then I'd rather it was pure.
I like it deep,
I like it shallow,
but I don't like it obscure.

So watch out for the shallow bits
where murky water lingers.
If you dive into
stuff like that,
you'll only break your fingers.

That Bad Alchemy

When I have grown fantastically old and rich
and dwell wizard-like in my enchanted castle

when I have mysteriously outlasted
all my rivals who for so long
seemed to be doing so much better

when all the women I have ever wanted
have also mysteriously outlived
those same rivals

when gradual rumours of my sorcery
and strange powers
are beginning to circulate freely

when one by one the women come
to see if perhaps
I'm not such a bad bet after all

I will pick up my crystal memories
those moments of rejection
like the seeds of bad living
lined up in neatly labelled jars

the memory for example
of standing stupid on your doorstep
listening to a stranger telling me
that you didn't live there anymore

and as you and so many others
turn back at last along the years
it will be your turn to knock upon my door
and my turn to not be at home.

There inside my castle I will sit
old rich and invisible beyond the slanted light
of narrow windows

listening as the unanswered knocks echo
from stone wall to stone wall
until even the echoes
give up in despair.

There inside my castle I will sit
proud bitter master yet servant to that alchemy
which turns love into anger:

an anger that is pure and true
and everlasting.

Welcome To The Tolerance Zone

We are happy to have you.
We are happy to have you stay.
We hope you are as happy to stay
as we are happy to have you stay.

Yes, welcome to the tolerance zone.
We are all happy to have each other
inside the tolerance zone.

We hope that you will not
attempt to leave.

The Right To Peace Of Mind

All law-abiding citizens
have the right to peace of mind:
to freedom from fear.

We will pass a law to imprison those
who interfere with this right.
All law-abiding citizens
will live in freedom from fear.

Only criminals need fear this new law.
We will imprison those criminals
who fear this law.

If you have any worries about this law,
please let us know.

From **An Exhibition Of The New Realism**

1: Use Of Appropriate Language

A politician, a baby, a garbage-crusher.

"It would be very easy, as we look at the smiling face of this baby, to say that we should not put it in the garbage-crusher. Even the mention of putting the baby in the garbage-crusher is likely to bring all the usual whining namby-pamby bleeding hearts out of the woodwork. But you should notice that these moaners who hawk their consciences so openly never themselves have to take responsibility for the important decisions that affect the future of our entire nation.

It may not be trendy or immediately popular to put this baby in the garbage-crusher; and it may not fit in neatly with whatever is the current fad in political correctness; but we of the elected government have to deal with the real world, and we would not be doing our duty to the country if we were to shy away from decisions which may be unpopular in the short term. And the fact is, today's babies need to be more flexible or they will simply be left behind, and it is only by putting this baby in the garbage-crusher that this baby can be made more flexible.

And it might help matters if, instead of moaning, those people were to take a more positive attitude towards putting this baby in the garbage-crusher. To those people I say: consider the alternative. If I do not crush this baby, Britain's position in the world will slide inexorably down and down, and then those same people will be moaning 'Oh, why didn't you put that baby in the garbage-crusher?' and 'Oh, how we wish you'd ignored us and put the baby in the garbage-crusher while there was still time.'

The fact is, that in years to come, those people will be thanking me for putting this baby in this garbage-crusher, for it is only by crushing this baby, and by crushing many other babies like it, that Britain can and will be made Great again."

2: The Golden Rules

Divide.
You can win with 40%
if the other 60% never get together.
For the 60%
use the stick and dangle the carrot.
Dangle the carrot
just close enough yet far enough away
that they never actually get hold of it.
Divide again.
Talk about the enemy within.
Use poverty and unemployment.
Let the bastards fight each other.
They will serve you well.
Oppress by gradualism.
Don't step up the attack
on too many people at once.
Keep the battle-lines moving.
Never let the 60% realize
they are all enemies within.
Take them by turn:
the trades unionists;
the miners;
the nurses;
the unemployed;
the unilateralists
the doctors;
the homosexuals;
the students;
the teachers;
the councillors;
the social workers;
the protesters;
the travellers;
the single mothers;
the homeless;
the young...

Take their money.
Take their rights.
Let them take their turn
to take the blame.
Make the worthless bastards squirm:
for those who are not for us,
we are against.

Rough Hollow Pearls In The Seaweed Night

It was the coast with the
most exploited labour: up to eighteen of us
at one time on fourteen miles of sand and mud:
mud spreading outwards on the marshes and flats,
and sand collapsing as the sea ate the dunes.
There were no terms and conditions;
or if there were, they were as shifting
as sand and mud.
At different times we were called
Employment Trainees
Adult Trainees
Employment Actionees
and Trainees For Work
as the Government played small games
with large numbers of people with no money.
This was the deal:
for dole plus ten pounds a week
which makes fifty pounds altogether
we would do work on the coast
be removed from the unemployment figures
and be called Trainees.
It has to be said that this work was varied.
Every Monday after the weekend crowds
we picked litter in the dunes
passing the time by trying to be the first to collect
a complete set of clothing at once:
in the absence of proper knickers,
a dirty nappy would count.
I tried to go one better and collect
a complete car as well,
but only ever managed it twice,
and neither of them worked.
We built and mended miles of fences,
built fences like building fences was the most trendiest thing
        on Earth:
post and rail, post and wire, birdsmouth, paling, brushwood.
We put sand-trapping fencing in front of the dunes
to build out the dunes each year
just to keep them in the same place.

We stood on the dunes at lunchtime
in the wind and sea-spray
and watched and laughed as the spring tides
destroyed our work for another year,
brown waves like giant hands clawing great fistfuls of sand,
and unto each generation of Trainees
shall go the destroyed work of the last.
We picked more litter,
planted marram
and then led school groups on dunes and beach, some discov-
     ering sea-shells for the first time.
We waded around natterjack breeding pools on fresh spring
     mornings searching out common toads and then drove
     thousands of them down the motorway to their new home in
     Wigan.
We picked more litter,
dug pools for natterjack toads, and carried tadpoles from
     drying-out pools to not-drying-out pools.
We surfaced footpaths with mulch, with wood, with stone,
surfaced footpaths like surfacing footpaths was the third most
     trendiest thing on Earth after litterpicking and building fences.
We picked more litter,
mended some more fences,
dressed up as vampires on Halloween,
sat bored for hours in the information caravan at fetes and
     shows,
put out dune fires with hoses, with spades, and, when we had
     to, with our hands and feet,
found lost children and stolen cars,
threw off poachers,
picked up more litter just for kicks and because the place was
     covered in it,
spent days on end cutting down sea buckthorn to stop it taking
     over the whole coast, and spent weeks on end getting the
     thorns out of our arms and legs after,
and picked up litter too.
Put in so many extra hours they turned into weeks but still got
     slagged off for laziness,
because we were the scum of the coast
floating around like an algal bloom
and after awhile we might get smelly.
One by one we are given our little pieces of paper,

turned back on the dole.
On the coast our departure is scarcely noticed:
by day the crowds come and go,
and new Trainees now take our places,
make new fences and repair those we made
till it is almost as if we were never there;
and later as we sit at home or spend what we can in the pub,
the ordinary darkness comes down like mist over the dunes,
and the waves in our absence
roll the empty shells of sea potatoes
gently on the sand,
laid like rough hollow pearls in the seaweed night.

Post-&-Wire Fencing Song

for use on employment training schemes

I've got work but I've got no pay.
I've got a job but no career.
What shall we do on this lovely day?
Let's build a fucking fence right here.

So drop the shuvvies in deep.
Grab and twist and lift and swing.
Drop the shuvvies in deep
For digging holes is a noble thing.

Heard about a man who once had a job
And every year made twenty grand.
Our pockets are full right up to the top
With sand and staples, staples and sand.

Tamp that ground real hard.
Whack that sand and make it ring.
Tamp that ground real hard
For tamping ground is a noble thing.

Pass me a post and stuff that strut.
Now I can see how our lives make sense:
We haven't got a wage so it can't be cut
So carry on building the post'n'wire fence.

Strain that wire real tight.
Pluck that wire and make it sing.
Strain that wire real tight
For straining wire is a noble thing.

Non-Executive Directing Poem

Daddy's in the government,
Our family's protector,
And when I grow up, I'll be
A non-executive director

For now he's done his bit
To privatize the public sector,
There are many posts that need
A non-executive director.

Mum says that only little men
Should pay the tax-collector;
And I'm gonna be a big,
Big, non-executive director.

It's my duty to the nation
And the public will respect a
Man who earns such giant sums
As non-executive director

For the job demands commitment
And I know I should expect a
Heavy workload when I start
As non-executive director

And twice a year at meetings
I'll turn up like Banquo's spectre
When I've grown up and become
A non-executive director.

You Don't Fuck With God

Well, God cursed Job one day,
     & killed his children & his flocks
& covered him in blisters
     from his stetson to his socks.
Job said to God, Hey God,
     that's a bit strong.
Would you mind letting on
     just what I did wrong?
& from out of the sky
     came a lengthy pause
Then a voice which proclaimed
     these heavenly laws:
Don't you dare question me,
     you puny little sod,
Cos I'm big & I'm strong,
     & you don't fuck with God.

Jesus hanging on the cross,
     called up to the sky,
& said Blimey dad, I'm well pissed off,
     I'm far too young to die.
God said, You want the reason
     why I left you in the lurch?
Well I don't like the way you treat
     the merchants in the church,
& I don't recall you ever asked
     or paid for no release
To go preaching all that hippy shit
     concerning love & peace.
You ever mess with me,
     you get a knee in the cod,
Cos I'm jealous as hell,
     & you don't fuck with God.

Johnny Snot at Sunday school
    said God, let's get this straight.
Is it only folks who ever
    disagree with you you hate?
But the bible's full of this & that:
    it's hard to tell what's what
So how the hell can people tell
    if they agree with you or not?
& God said Shut your fucking face
    you scruffy little git.
Do you think my contradictions
    make me give a single shit?
For my ways are mysterious:
    in fact they're bloody odd.
I'm ineffable, & that means
    you don't fuck with God.

Surrealist Haiku

The pen of my aunt
Is blue. Distantly she hears
The honking of geese.

Rebel Haiku

Critics dislike you
If you write rhyming haiku.
Imagine their whines

At a haiku with four lines.

Recollections In Tranquility

Now, some poets type, but instead,
I do my writing all in my head,
Thus I can compose
All my poems and prose
Without once getting up out of bed.

New Year's Resolution

I have decided to marshal my thoughts.
From now on
I shall think neat thoughts in neat formations.
I shall at last set my mind in order.
I shall think purposeful and well-drilled thoughts,
Battalions of thoughts that know exactly where they're going
And exactly how to get there.
No more scruffy and undisciplined thoughts
Turned out sloppily on parade again.
I want thoughts with buttons that sparkle,
Thoughts that stand straight-backed at attention,
Thoughts with boots so shiny that I can see my own reflection
    in them:
My shiny new reflection;
For this new neatness in my thoughts will of course be reflec-
    ted in my outward appearance.
People will look at me and say:
"Look. There is a man with a mind like a parade ground
And thoughts like a crack commando unit,
Thoughts that deserve medals."
Yes, I shall have thoughts that deserve medals.
All of my thoughts will deserve the D.C.M. at least,
Because thoughts which do not deserve medals
Will not be admitted.
Thoughts which do not deserve medals
Will be shot.
I'm going to sort out the men-thoughts
From the boy-thoughts,
And give the boy-thoughts all a thorough lesson in growing
    up.
I'm going to learn to tell the sheep-thoughts
From the goat-thoughts,
And then get rid of both,
Neither sheep nor goats being suitable recruitment material
For the mental army of tomorrow.
Sheep are woolly-minded cowards
And goats are notorious for their lack of discipline
And neither are shiny.
Any sheep or goats found inside my mind will be expelled

And a 200 millimetre exclusion zone will be set up
Within which all thoughts will be vigorous, healthy, neat, dis-
    ciplined and totally unsheeplike and ungoatlike.
Some people do not mind having minds full of sheeplike and
    goatlike thoughts.
Some people just let their thoughts wander all over the place
    for most of the time,
Thoughts wandering like herds of sheep and goats grazing
uncontrolled and eating almost anything,
Thoughts that follow each other all over the show with no
    thought for where the first thought is leading them,
Rogue thoughts roaming at large and devouring things they
    oughtn't be devouring just now,
Devouring things they oughtn't be devouring at all:
Trousers, for example.
Everyone knows that goatlike thoughts will eat trousers at the
    slightest provocation.
Even razorwire-sharp starched creases offer no protection
    from roaming goatlike thoughts,
And the trousers are mercilessly attacked and devoured:
Once-proud trousers reduced to mere food for goatlike
    thoughts.
And then the chickens!
Chicken-thoughts pecking everywhere and leaving chickenshit
    all over the parade ground,
Butterfly-thoughts fluttering in aimless abandon and badger-
    thoughts galloping all over the parade-ground, badger-
    thoughts building setts to live in in the Do-Not-Walk-On
    grass and kicking up the earth like it was all some sort of game.
Some people have minds not like a parade ground at all, minds
instead like a cross between a farmyard and a jungle!
Minds full of chicken-thoughts squawking everywhere amongst
    the wandering sheep-thoughts and rooting badger-thoughts,
Butterfly-thoughts fluttering all around the terrible trouser-
    eating goat-thoughts.
What can you do with someone who has a mind like a free-
    range menagerie?
People with so much thoughtspace taken up by thoughts that
    needn't be there at all?
If people like that ever do have a useful idea it's as likely as
    not it's not even the one they were looking for in the first place.
How can anyone develop a strategy for life with all this free-

range animal liberation stuff going on in their head all the
time?
How can I plan the tactics of tomorrow with a headful of wild
wildlife circus?
I have decided to marshal my thoughts
Immediately.
From now on
I shall think neat thoughts in neat formations,
Badgers and goats permitting.
I shall at last set my mind in order,
Sheep and butterflies permitting,
And depending on the chickens.
I have decided to marshal my thoughts
Immediately
As soon as things quieten down a little.

IRON Press was formed in Spring 1973, initially to publish the magazine IRON which more than two decades, and more than 1,500 writers on, survives as one of the country's most active alternative mags – a fervent purveyor of new poetry, fiction and graphics. £12.00 gets you a subscription. Try our intriguing book list too, titles which can rarely be found on the shelves of mega-stores. Fortified by a belief in good writing, as against literary competitions or marketing trivia, IRON remains defiantly a small press. Our address is at the front of this book